T0122145

I LOVE FRUITS

Becky Boo

Copyright © 2018 by Becky Boo. 780049

ISBN: Softcover   978-1-5434-0953-6
         EBook   978-1-5434-0952-9

All rights reserved. No part of this book may be
reproduced or transmitted in any form or by
any means, electronic or mechanical, including
photocopying, recording, or by any information
storage and retrieval system, without permission in
writing from the copyright owner.

Print information available on the last page

Rev. date: 05/30/2018

To order additional copies of this book, contact:
Xlibris
1-800-455-039
www.xlibris.com.au
Orders@Xlibris.com.au

I LOVE FRUITS

I like Apples

I like Pears

I like Bananas

I like Berries

I like Watermelons

I Love Fruits

Comparisons

I am Good

I am Better

I am Beautiful

I am More Beautiful

At The Beach

I like
playing in the sand

I like
playing in the water

I like playing
with the shells

I love playing
at the Beach

Printed in the United States
By Bookmasters